ECOSYSTEMS

Life on an Ocean Shore

Stuart A. Kallen

**KIDHAVEN
PRESS™**

THOMSON
™
GALE

San Diego • Detroit • New York • San Francisco • Cleveland
New Haven, Conn. • Waterville, Maine • London • Munich

THOMSON
GALE

For more information, contact
KidHaven Press
27500 Drake Rd.
Farmington Hills, MI 48331-3535
Or you can visit our Internet site at http://www.gale.com

LIBRARY OF CONGRESS CATALOGING-IN-PUBLICATION DATA

Kallen, Stuart A., 1955–
  Life on an ocean shore / by Stuart A. Kallen.
    v. cm. — (Ecosystems)
Includes bibliographical references (p.   ).
Contents: The world of the waves — Plants along the ocean shore — Creatures in the sea — Creatures from the land.
  ISBN 0-7377-1531-6 (hardback : alk. paper)
  1. Seashore ecology—Juvenile literature. [1. Seashore ecology. 2. Ecology.]
I. Title. II. Series.
  QH541.5.S35 K36 2003
  577.69'9—dc21
                                      2002153657

Contents

Chapter 1

The Intertidal Zone

Ocean shores are areas of sand and rock that act as a buffer between the land and the sea. These coastlines are constantly shaped and reshaped by winds, weather, and **tides**. Foamy waves that endlessly break on the shore shift sands and crumble rocks. Ocean breezes gradually create sand dunes and sculpt the sheer faces of cliffs. And severe storms such as monsoons and hurricanes can rearrange thousands of acres of shoreline within a few hours.

Seventy percent of the earth is covered by the sea, and ocean shores ring all continents and islands. Scientists divide these coastlines into five broad zones: tropical coasts, desert coasts, warm temperate coasts, cool temperate coasts, and polar coasts. Each zone has its own unique environmental factors that are affected by the climate. Tropical coasts in South America, for example, are known for their warm and rainy weather. The barren polar coasts near the North and South Poles are lined with ice packs and glaciers that continually crumble into the sea.

Whatever sort of **environment** exists along the ocean shore, coastlines are classified as either sandy beaches, rocky coasts, or wetlands such as tidal flats

This coral reef is part of a tropical coast, one of the five coastal zones found around the world.

and salt marshes. And all of these **ecosystems** are strongly affected by the periodic rise and fall of ocean waters known as the tides.

The Tides

Tides are caused by the moon's natural force of attraction called gravity. When oceans face the moon, gravity pulls on the water and creates a dome of water that bulges away from the land. This creates low tides at

Giant icebergs are stranded on the rocky coast near the North Pole during a low tide.

seashores. When land faces the moon, the ocean is pulled toward the shore, creating high tides. As the earth turns on its axis once every twenty-four hours, most places experience two high tides and two low tides. Every day along coastlines the ocean rises for about six hours, falls for about six hours, and then rises and falls again.

The narrow belt of ocean shore that lies between the lowest and highest tides is called the **intertidal zone**. This area is underwater during high tides and exposed to various degrees of wind and sun during

low tides. Thousands of species of plants and animals make their homes within this ever changing ecosystem washed by the waves.

Sandy Beaches

Almost all ocean shores are shaped by the tides but flat sandy beaches are altered more rapidly than any other coastal environment. Sand is actually composed of very tiny grains of rocks, minerals, black lava, seashells, mud, coral, and other elements that have been pounded into small fragments by wind, water, and waves. When a wave breaks on a shore, it may carry sand from the ocean floor and deposit it on the beach. Large waves, however, can scour sand from the beaches and carry it out to sea. This process, called **erosion**, may be very dramatic. The sandy beach at Carmel, California, for example, is about two hundred feet wide in July. On stormy days in autumn and winter, powerful crashing waves carry away as much as six feet of sand a day and the shoreline becomes a rocky coast. In spring and summer, gentle waves and currents dredge the sand from the ocean floor and rebuild the beach.

In some areas where strong winds continually blow in from the sea, huge hills of sand, called sand dunes, are formed. These piles of sand are ever changing and over the course of thousands of years can move far inland. Along the thirteen-hundred-mile desert coast in Namibia, Africa, winds have built the tallest sand dunes in the world, up to eight hun-

What Causes High and Low Tides?

① The moon's gravity pulls Earth's sea waters, creating a tidal bulge. This bulge causes the sea level to rise, resulting in a high tide in the waters facing the moon.

② Because the sea waters opposite the moon are least affected by the moon's gravity, these waters bulge away from the moon. This causes a high tide in the waters opposite the moon.

③ As the moon orbits Earth, the tidal bulges rotate in the direction of the moon. Each day Earth experiences two high tides and two low tides.

④ In between the two tidal bulges the water level must drop. These areas of lower sea level are low tides.

dred feet high. This shoreline is so bone dry and desolate that it is called the Skeleton Coast for the skeletons of wrecked ships and sailors that littered the sands over the centuries. The massive dunes of the Skeleton Coast are pockmarked with peaks, swirls, and ridges that give them the appearance of ocean waves made from sand.

The Rocky Coast

Most beaches have sections, known as rocky coasts, where the sand gives way to spectacular towering cliffs. Waves along a rocky coast can pound craggy boulders and cliffs with a force equal to a car driving into a stone wall at ninety miles per hour. As a result, some rocky coasts are eroded at a rate of five or six feet a year. As this happens, caves are formed as chunks break off and fall, leaving a beach strewn with various sized pieces of rubble. This debris is made of fragments that may be as big as houses or as small as pebbles. In some areas, such as the Orkney Islands in Scotland, huge pillars of rock, called sea stacks, are formed from old pieces of crumbled cliffs that are now marooned offshore.

Like sandy beaches, conditions along rocky coasts are influenced by wind, waves, and weather. Conditions change hour to hour, day to day, and season to season as the tides rise and fall and cascading waves break, splash, churn, and carve solid rock.

At low tide, it is possible to walk along rocky shores, stepping over the jagged rocks. At high tide, rocky coasts are often submerged as waves pound directly into the cliffs. Day after day, these waves create caves, holes, and narrow trenches under the cliffs, weakening them. When storms, earthquakes, or heavy rains occur, the cliffs can collapse, causing rockslides that bury whatever is below.

Rocky coasts are also dangerous to ships. In the northwestern Hawaiian Islands, for example, centuries of storms and high waves have created a ship graveyard where hundreds of vessels have sunk in the rock-studded waters. In some places anchors, chains, rigging, and other equipment of ancient whaling ships litter the ocean floor.

Barrier Islands

Other ocean shores, such as **barrier islands**, are more welcoming to sea travelers. These long, narrow islands are made from sand and lie parallel to sandy beaches. They are so named because they absorb the impact of incoming waves and act as barriers to protect the sandy beaches behind them. Some of these sandbars may be very large. The Great Barrier Island north of Auckland, New Zealand, is almost twenty-five miles long and ten miles wide. About a dozen towns filled

Rocky coasts like this one are dangerous during heavy storms, and can become graveyards for ships as well as people.

Parts of a Barrier Island

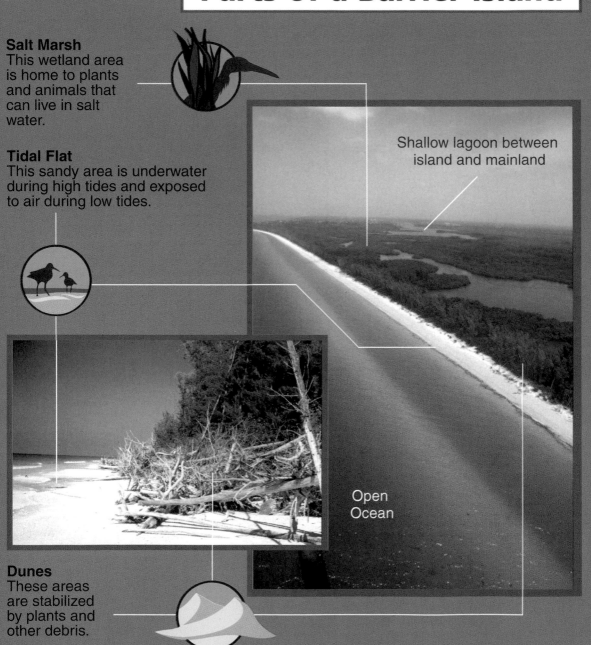

Salt Marsh
This wetland area is home to plants and animals that can live in salt water.

Tidal Flat
This sandy area is underwater during high tides and exposed to air during low tides.

Shallow lagoon between island and mainland

Open Ocean

Dunes
These areas are stabilized by plants and other debris.

with restaurants, motels, shops, roads, and airstrips dot the sandbar.

Flats and Marshes

Tidal flats and salt marshes form along the shore in the area between a barrier island and the mainland. Tidal flats are simply sandy areas that are underwater at high tide and exposed to air at low tide. Marshes are wetlands, like swamps and lagoons, that contain plants and animals that can survive in salty ocean water.

Whether a region consists of a sandy beach, a rocky coast, or a marshy wetland, the ocean's continual pounding carves the ocean shore into a countless array of nooks and crannies. This is clearly seen on the Pacific coastline of the United States. If a person were to fly along the coast from Mexico to Canada, they would cover a distance of four thousand miles. If they walked along every twist and turn of the ocean shore, across coves and inlets and bays, they would travel a distance of fifty-six thousand miles. And in this region where the land meets the sea, they would observe some of the most beautiful and dramatic scenery found anywhere in the world.

Chapter 2

Plants Along the Ocean Shore

The ocean shore is a fascinating world that is part land and part sea. Although it is pounded by waves, baked by the sun, dried by the wind, and, in some places, frozen by the snow, the intertidal zone hosts a wide variety of plant life. But survival is difficult in this ever changing environment. Some plants need air to survive but remain underwater during times of high tide. Other plants depend on seawater, but are exposed to the drying effects of air and sun at low tide. Storms lash beaches, tossing boulders about and smothering plants under sand. Other plants are ripped from the ocean floor by their roots. And those that survive nature's violence may live only to be eaten by sea creatures. Despite this harsh environment, ocean shores contain a tremendous variety of habitats and support a rich and complex web of interconnected plant and animal life.

Important Plankton

The most abundant plants along the ocean shore are microscopic one-celled plants called diatoms, or **phytoplankton**. These plants are a type of algae that are so small, one thousand could fit on the head

Billions of phytoplankton (inset) wash ashore during a red tide on Canada's east coast.

of a pin and 10 million may be found in only a quart of seawater. Although they are tiny, plankton are the most important plants on Earth. Small fish, and some species of whales, eat them. Larger fish then eat the smaller fish. Humans catch and eat many of these larger fish. Thus, the plankton are an important part of the food chain.

Billions of plankton wash ashore with every wave, coating rocks and sand with a living green glaze that also feeds shore creatures such as barnacles, mussels, and countless other animals.

Even in death, the diatoms provide energy for humanity. As trillions of plankton die, they are buried under the ocean sands. Over millions of years, these diatoms have packed down into pools that eventually become petroleum. As a result, ocean shores throughout the world are rich in oil reserves that are extracted for use in gasoline, asphalt, and industrial products.

Forests of Kelp

While tiny diatoms help support all life on Earth, one of the earth's longest plants, giant kelp, also plays an important roll in the ecology of ocean shores. Giant kelp is a type of seaweed that grows in the waters off California, Tasmania, and elsewhere. These plants develop in thick groves, called forests, in offshore waters about sixty feet deep. Although submerged, the kelp's leaves reach upward to catch the life-giving sunlight that penetrates the water. Some giant kelp can grow up to three hundred feet long, the length of

A southern fur seal plunges into the water above a kelp forest.

a football field. In fact, the giant kelp is sometimes referred to as the "sequoia of the sea," since it measures about the same length as the giant sequoia trees in the California mountains.

Long strands of kelp float near the ocean's surface, buoyed by small bubbles in its stems that are filled with oxygen—the same principle that allows a beach ball to float in the water. The plant's long, ropy, copper-colored stems are anchored to the ocean floor with powerful roots called holdfasts.

Like a forest on land, a kelp forest is home to many animals. This offshore habitat swarms with millions of creatures, some as large as the angel shark, others as small as the tiny brine shrimp. In shallow waters, sea urchins graze on kelp leaves like rabbits munch let-

The hardy kelp seaweed (pictured) grows in thick groves, and can reach lengths of three hundred feet.

tuce. And these kelp beds act as nurseries for the eggs of fish, jellyfish, sea urchins, crabs, and other creatures. These busy sea environments can rival tropical rain forests in their color, abundance, and variety of life. In fact, the kelp beds may have at least 750 species of fish, squid, **crustaceans**, and other sea life living in them.

When winter storms rip kelp from their moorings, the plants wash onshore with the tides and provide feasts for crowds of crustaceans such as lobsters and crabs that scramble along the shore.

Chemicals in kelp also provide products that people use every day. In countries throughout the world, special machines harvest kelp leaves which are used to produce a gelatin-like product called algin. This substance is used to make ice cream, lipstick, toothpaste, and other goods. It is even used to make clothing dye.

A Variety of Colors

There are hundreds of other species of seaweed with as many colors as a rainbow. Bright red *callac* looks like a dinner salad, while the stringy *chocae* is bluish purple. Rockweeds, or sea wracks, wave their rubbery greenish brown leaves in the water during high tides and lay flat like matted hair during low tides. Reddish brown Irish moss, mixed with bright green sea lettuce is exposed to air only every few weeks when the tide is at its lowest monthly ebb.

Seaweed is also utilized in dozens of products including shaving cream, rubber, paint, and fertilizer. The plants are even a popular addition to Japanese cooking when dried and made into nori, *kombu*, *wakame*, and other foods.

Lichens

Lichens are another plant species that can grow under harsh conditions along the rocky coasts. Lichens turn lifeless rocks into tiny gardens of red, brown, green, orange, white, and blue that may change color several times during a single day. For example, when the salt spray of a high tide washes over rock tripe, the plant appears as a soft mat of green. When the tide recedes, the hot sun bakes the plant into a blackened crust until the tide returns once more.

The bright orange wall lichen can spread up cliffs and boulders, surviving underwater during the highest tides. Like all lichens, this plant attaches itself to bare rock and emits a powerful acid from its roots that dissolves even hard granite into tiny particles of dirt. This allows moss, grasses, and even trees to gain a foothold on barren rocks along the ocean shore.

With about twenty thousand different species, lichens can take on many shapes. They may look like layers of peeling paint or leafy emerald plants. Trees that grow near the ocean in cool temperate coasts are often colonized by a long, hairlike lichen known as old man's beard that hangs down from the branches like wispy whiskers.

Lichens grow extremely slowly, spreading out at less than an inch per year. They are some of the oldest plants on Earth. The lichens growing along the

Coconut palms grow near the high tide line and use the ocean to spread their seeds (inset) from coast to coast.

frozen coast of western Greenland are over forty-five hundred years old.

Shore Trees

While specially adapted plants grow in the intertidal zone, nearly every sort of plant may be found thriving just out of the ocean's reach, above the high tide line. In warm climates ocean shores are ringed with an astonishing variety of wildflowers, bushes, vines, and other plants.

Along tropical coasts, coconut palms are a common sight. These trees produce hard, brown coconuts that can float on the sea for months. In this way the coconut spreads its seed from beach to beach, sometimes hundreds or thousands of miles from its original habitat.

Some of the oldest and largest trees in the world may be found in the wet and rainy temperate coastal zones of the Pacific Northwest. Sitka spruce, up to two hundred feet tall, grow right down to the high tide mark in the misty forests of British Columbia, Canada. Towering Douglas fir, found in the same region, may live to be twelve hundred years old. While many such trees have been cut down and processed into lumber and paper, environmentalists have been fighting to save what remains of these old growth forests.

From the tops of swaying pines waving in the clear blue sky to the microscopic plankton, thousands of species of plants make the harsh environment of the ocean shore rich with life.

Chapter 3

Creatures of the Intertidal Zone

The ocean shore, whether it is a sand beach or rocky coast, is teeming with life that creeps, crawls, and skitters along between the tide lines. Some shore residents, such as birds, make their homes on the land. But crabs, lobsters, periwinkles, and other crustaceans depend on the ocean to survive.

Creatures that live in the intertidal zone face several challenges. As the tides move out, they must protect themselves from the harmful drying effects of the wind and the sun. More troublesome are the predators, especially birds, who thrive on seafood. Add strong currents, storms, wind, rain, and snow, and animals that live on the edge of the sea face daily battles with the fickle whims of nature.

Zones of Life on a Rocky Coast

Each different animal species found along the ocean shore has developed its own way of dealing with periodic exposure to air and water. This is most clearly seen along rocky areas of temperate coasts where four separate zones between high and low tide are stacked up like a set of stairs. Each level, or zone, is alive with unique communities of creatures.

The area of rocks highest up on the shoreline is called the periwinkle or splash zone. Sprayed with seawater only during the highest tides, this zone is named for the small sea snails called periwinkles that thrive in this part of the shoreline, grazing on the dusky blue-green algae that blankets the rocks. In order to survive in this harsh environment between land and sea, the half-inch periwinkle emits a gluelike mucous called holdfast that anchors it to rocks even as the cascading waves break over its shell. When feeding, the tiny periwinkle can walk up to thirty feet between tide cycles, pulling itself along on one slimy foot. And if they are accidentally washed into the ocean, these periwinkles can endure beneath the water for three months. They can be exposed to air for an equal length of time before drying out.

In the area below the periwinkle zone, the barnacle zone bears the heaviest brunt of the breaking waves. This area is exposed to air twice a day for a few hours when the tide is out. As the tides shift, hard-shell barnacles glue themselves to rocks where they can remain

The splash zone provides a safe haven for tiny periwinkle snails that feed on the blue-green algae that grows here.

for up to five years. When the tide is out, they shut their shells tightly and remain motionless. But when covered with seawater, barnacles spring open and extend six pairs of feathery legs that grab passing plankton, which they stuff into their mouths. Although few creatures can survive in the ever changing environment between land and sea, barnacles thrive. In some places, so many of these shelled creatures attach themselves to the rocks that they smother each other, resulting in a high death rate.

The barnacle's hard shell is no match for the meat-eating snail called the dog whelk, however. Whelks simply rip holes in barnacle shells with a drill-like rib-

Zones of a Rocky Coast

1 Splash Zone
This area is sprayed with seawater only during high tides. Periwinkles feed on the moss and algae that grow here.

2 Barnacle Zone
This area is exposed to air twice a day during low tides. Barnacles and the predatory dog whelk live here.

3 Rockweed Zone
This area is exposed to air only during the lowest tides and is home to mussels and limpets.

4 Kelp Zone
This area is the lowest zone and is rarely exposed to air. A variety of ocean creatures lives here.

bon of teeth. After injecting a powerful poison, the dog whelk uses its raspy teeth to feast on the soft shrimplike barnacle inside.

Life in the Low Zones

The middle shore or rockweed zone is a wetter environment below the barnacle zone that is exposed to air about half the time. And when the tide is out, countless creatures hide beneath the ropy seaweed located here.

The middle shore is home to the limpet, which looks like a slug with a tiny turtle shell on its back. Limpets attach themselves to rocks during low tides, but move off to feed when the water returns. As the tide recedes again, the limpet moves back to the exact same spot on the rock and attaches itself to its "home." Mussels also join themselves permanently to rocks in this zone, using strong threads to hold tight.

The lower shore, or kelp zone, is the lowest zone very close to the sea, and is almost constantly covered with seawater. It is only exposed to air and sun several times a month when the tides are at their lowest ebb. Among the holdfast roots of the kelp, this area is crawling with life. Starfish pull themselves along with hundreds of suction cups, called tube feet, on their five arms. They smother mussels and snails and devour their victims through a mouth located in the center of their starry body.

Crabs hide under rocks at low tide and act as the scavengers of the shore, feeding on chunks of seaweed

The carnivorous sea anemone uses its deadly tentacles to capture and paralyze prey.

and seafood that float by. Crabs grab this food and pull it into their mouths with powerful claws that can give a painful pinch to anyone who tries to pick them up.

The kelp zone is also home to the sea anemone, a creature that looks like a plant but is really a meat-eating animal. Anemones, which attach themselves to rocks, come in many shapes and sizes and are colored brilliant white, bright pink, fluorescent green, and many other colors. And their waving tentacles look like beautiful underwater flowers. Any animal that mistakes this sea creature for a passive plant, however, quickly becomes dinner when the anemone uses its deadly tentacles to shoot poison into its victim before eating it.

Tide Pools

In all areas but the kelp zone, puddles of seawater called tide pools form in holes, cracks, and crevasses between the rocks. These tidal pools hold enough seawater to support marine life even as the surrounding area dries when the tide recedes.

Tide pools are like the ocean in miniature. Lush beds of seaweed line the pool crevice providing shelter and food for fish, sponges, crabs, sea anemones, sea slugs, mussels, starfish, and others that live together in the temporarily calm waters. On clear nights, tide pools

A dazzling green sea slug explores the shallow waters of a tide pool.

may reflect the starry skies, and also glow with luminous algae that emit low levels of bluish light. During the day, beachcombers may be found sitting beside tide pools watching the underwater drama in a natural aquarium.

Life is not easy for the tide pool communities, however. These areas warm quickly in the sun and can evaporate over the course of a few hours, leaving struggling animals to die. And for hungry predators, shallow pools are great places to find food. For example, snails trapped in a tide pool with a starfish have little means of escape and prove an easy meal for the five-armed marine creature.

Supporting Sea Life

While many sea creatures live in the intertidal zone, some come to shore only for breeding purposes. Every year between May and October, three-hundred-pound loggerhead sea turtles crawl out of the ocean in the dark of night to nest along the east coast of Mexico. Here, the turtles dig holes with their large flippers and lay about one hundred soft, leathery eggs. After covering the eggs with sand, the mother turtles crawl back through the surf zone and disappear into the deep sea.

About two months later, dozens of baby turtles, called hatchlings, poke through their shells and head straight for the surf as soon as they are born. Before they get to the ocean, however, they must skitter past hundreds of screeching seagulls, herons, raccoons, and others who grab the hatchlings for a quick meal.

A mother loggerhead sea turtle deposits her eggs in a sandy shoreline nest.

After leaving their nest, loggerhead sea turtle hatchlings scurry toward the shore.

The few survivors who make it to the water, however, can live over one hundred years.

Although the ocean shore looks like a peaceful place, life can be short and brutal for creatures who live in the intertidal zone. Whether it is a starfish devouring a snail or a whelk rasping apart a barnacle, every creature has its enemies as well as a way to defend itself in this harsh environment beneath the waves.

Chapter 4

Creatures from the Land

The seashore is home to hundreds of species that make their homes in the intertidal zone. The ocean shore also attracts a wide variety of land animals that depend on shoreline habitat for survival.

Graceful, long-winged seagulls are the most common creatures along the ocean shore. Beach visitors often see them circling overhead, screeching at one another and begging for morsels of food from picnickers and fishermen.

Flying, Fishing, and Feeding

In addition to seagulls, hundreds of bird species, known as shorebirds, live at the seashore seasonally or year-round. These birds often perch in the rocks and

Shorebirds such as seagulls and pelicans (inset) depend on the intertidal zone for food.

cliffs above the tide line and depend on creatures that live in the ocean or intertidal zone for survival.

Pelicans, found on coastlines throughout the world, are perhaps the best fishermen among the seabirds. In California, brown pelicans can be seen diving headfirst into the sea and scooping up fish with their huge bills. The white pelican of Texas and Florida has a different fishing technique, however. These birds work in teams, swimming in groups in the sea, rounding up fish like cowboys herd cattle.

Once the fish are trapped, the birds use their pouch-like beaks to grab them.

The most dramatic seabird predator may be the osprey, also known as the fish hawk, found along coasts in both North and South America. With a wingspan of more than five feet and four razor-sharp talons on each foot, these birds of prey hunt over a wide distance. When an osprey sees a fish, the bird will hover above until it is ready to strike. At the right moment, the osprey dives, its wings half closed and its eight talons extended. With a great swoosh of water, the osprey disappears momentarily under the sea only to emerge a few seconds later with the slippery wriggling fish in its claws. When the osprey lands, it will hold the fish with one foot while tearing it apart with its powerful beak. Then the bird will eat the parts, devouring the head first.

A hungry osprey holds a fish with one foot before devouring the animal with its powerful beak.

While ospreys depend on superb flying skills, penguins use their stubby wings to swim after fish and other prey. Penguins are usually associated with the polar coast of Antarctica, but millions of these flightless birds may be found in the warmer climates of Australia, New Zealand, South Africa, and even the Galápagos Islands near the equator.

The Adélie penguin is the most common, and the smallest, of these flightless birds. About 5 million of these creatures live on the icy shores of Antarctica. Where large colonies are gathered, a parade of penguins may be seen leaping off the shoreline ice into the sea. Sometimes leopard seals wait beneath the ice, catching the Adélies in their hungry jaws as they jump into the water.

Seals

In Antarctica and elsewhere, large, furry seals are nearly as common as seagulls. On ocean shores throughout the world, seals can be seen basking in the sun on sandbars, rocks, docks, and beaches. On the East Coast of the United States, harbor seals can weigh more than 250 pounds and exceed five feet in length. On the West Coast, elephant seals grow much larger; males can exceed twenty-one feet and weigh up to five thousand pounds.

Elephant seals were hunted to near extinction in the last century, as each one could provide nearly two hundred gallons of oil, which was used to produce lamp oil, soap, and other products. Today the animals

Curious emperor penguins get a closer look at a juvenile fur seal.

are endangered because of water pollution and loss of habitat.

Along the Skeleton Coast of Africa, nearly 2 million fur seals live in large colonies on small, rocky islands and sandy beaches. These animals, also known as golden seals, are ferocious hunters that tear through large schools of fish and can dive down to six hundred feet below the surface to chase squid. Seals, however, face extinction by humans who kill tens of thousands of the pups for their light-colored fur.

Pollution from garbage and chemicals causes great harm to the ocean and the animals that depend on it.

Pollution Problems

In addition to overhunting, millions of animals that live along the ocean shore are harmed by air and water pollution, overfishing, and increasing development.

With hundreds of millions of people living, working, and playing along ocean shores, coastal regions have been flooded with paper, plastic, aluminum cans, and other trash. In fact, people dump more than 14 billion tons of garbage into the ocean every year, including 650,000 plastic bottles every day. Carried by the tides and currents, much of this debris washes up on seashores sooner or later. Seabirds, turtles, and other creatures mistake plastic bags, balloons, and Styrofoam packing pellets for food. The populations of least fifty different species of seabirds have been reduced by eating this trash. Baby seals are sometimes seen on beaches snarled in cast-off fishing nets and other plastic debris. And otters, seagulls, and other animals are strangled when six-pack holders accidentally become entangled around their necks.

Chemical pollution and oil spills are also major problems. In November 2002, an oil tanker broke apart and sank off the coast of Spain in one of the world's richest fishing grounds. The ship released about 5 million gallons of toxic black fuel oil that washed up on Spanish shores in an oil slick seventy miles long and five miles wide. This accident caused immeasurable harm to the beaches in the region and killed thousands of fish, lobsters, seabirds, and other creatures. While such huge oil spills are uncommon, at least fifteen to twenty major oil tanker accidents occur near shore every year.

Threats from Global Warming

Air pollution is also harming the ecology of the ocean shores. Satellite surveys have detected a sharp decline in plankton in several of the world's oceans. Scientists trace this problem to **global warming**, which is caused by an increasing level of pollution from cars, factories, and industrial agriculture. Since plankton needs cool water to thrive, warming oceans have caused plankton levels to fall as much as 30 percent in some places since the 1980s.

Global warming is also blamed for rising sea levels over the past century. Many scientists believe that warming is causing the polar ice caps to melt, and ocean levels are expected to continue to rise. The ocean shores of today are expected to be swamped by the tides in the coming years as the sea continues to advance onto the land. As the ocean continues to pound the shore, no matter how much effort people apply to stemming the flow of the tides, the restless ocean will always claim the beaches, rocky shores, and even houses, highways, and cities that lay in its path.

Glossary

barrier island: Long, narrow, sand islands that lie parallel to beaches and act as protective barriers by absorbing the impact of the waves.

crustacean: A variety of aquatic creatures that include lobsters, crabs, shrimps, and barnacles.

ecosystem: A community of plants and animals, together with its environment, functioning as a unit.

environment: The combination of conditions that affect and influence the growth, development, and survival of plants and animals.

erosion: The process of wind, water, and other forces wearing away material from the earth's surface.

global warming: The gradual rising of the earth's temperature due to air pollution, which traps the sun's heat close to the planet's surface.

intertidal zone: The narrow belt of ocean shore that lies between the high and low tide lines.

phytoplankton: Microscopic, one-celled plants that float near the surface in fresh or salt water and serve as food for fish and other larger animals.

tide: The periodic rise and fall of ocean waters governed by the gravitational pull of the moon. At high tide, ocean waters rise to their highest point on the shoreline. At ebb tide, the waters sink to their lowest.

For Further Exploration

Books

Kathy Darling, *Seashore Babies*. New York: Walker, 1997. This book contains photographs and facts about infant seals, pelicans, turtles, crabs, and other coastal creatures.

Marcia S. Gresko, *Tide Pools*. San Diego: KidHaven, 2001. This book explores the amazing plants and peculiar animals found in tide pools along the ocean shore.

Kris Hirschmann, *Sea Stars*. San Diego: KidHaven, 2002. The sea stars' habitat, anatomy, feeding habits, and life cycles are the focus of this delightful book.

W. Wright Robinson, *How Shellmakers Build Their Amazing Homes*. San Diego: Blackbirch, 1999. This book looks at the watery world of mollusks and the techniques they use to create their beautiful shells.

Donald M. Silver, *One Small Square: Seashore*. New York: W.H. Freeman, 1993. The unique creatures, plants, and ecology found in a small area of an ocean shore are examined in this book.

Websites

Corrina Chase and Nancy Chase, **The Tide Pool Page**, Oregon State University Hatfield Marine Science Center, (http://hmsc.orst.edu). A site with useful information about tide pools along with photo and drawing links to the dozens of plants and animals typically found in these natural aquariums.

Craig C. Freudenrich, **How Barrier Islands Work**, (http://science.howstuffworks.com). This website explores the ecosystems of barrier islands, how they form, and threats to their survival.

Allison Hill, **Why Tides?** (www.sfgate.com). A site with an informative animation that explains how tides affect the ocean.

Index

About the Author

Stuart A. Kallen is the author of more than 150 nonfiction books for children and young adults. He has written on topics ranging from the theory of relativity to the history of rock and roll. In addition, Mr. Kallen has written award-winning children's videos and television scripts. In his spare time, Stuart A. Kallen is a singer/songwriter/guitarist in San Diego, California.